NAVIGATING ROUGH S.E.A.S.

SOUL ERODING ASSIMILATION-FORCING SYSTEMS

A GUIDED RECLAMATION JOURNAL

DR. TONICIA FREEMAN–FOSTER

ISBN: 979-8-9898669-3-9

Printed in the United States of America

Disclaimer Notice

The information in this guided reclamation journal should not be used for diagnosing or treating a health problem or disease. Those seeking personal medical advice should consult a licensed physician or mental health professional. Always consult your doctor or a qualified health provider regarding any medical conditions.

If you think you may have a medical or mental health emergency, call 911 or go to the nearest emergency room immediately. By your continued use of this guided reclamation journal and resources, you acknowledge that Dr. Tonicia Freeman-Foster ("Author") and PURPOSEFUL SUCCESS LLC dba LEIDOSWEL® ("Company") comments and recommendations about any outcome are expressions of opinion only, are neither promises nor guarantees, and will not be construed as promises or guarantees of any kind or of any sort. The Author and Company's sole guarantee is that the Author and Company will render this guided journal in accordance with the terms as set forth on the website.

The reproduction, scanning, uploading, photocopying, and electronic transmission of any part of this guided reclamation journal shall not be reproduced without the permission of the Author.

The Author and Company have made every effort to verify the information provided is accurate as of the date of publication. The Author does not assume any responsibility for any errors or omissions that may appear in this guided reclamation journal.

Hello!

Thank you for your purchase! I am Dr. Tonicia Freeman-Foster, also known as Dr. T. or Dr. TF². I'm the best-selling author of Navigating Rough S.E.A.S. — Soul Eroding Assimilation-Forcing Systems. I serve as the Co-Founder & CEO of LEIDOSWEL (pronounced lead-us-well)—a national firm specializing in leadership development coaching and consulting experiences for mid- to executive-level leaders and entrepreneurs nationally.

I'm excited to offer this guided reclamation journal as a reflective and action-oriented companion to the book. This journal has been created intentionally and thoughtfully with love. The goal of this journal is to support you in locating yourself, identifying who you were created to be, and embracing your journey through affirmations, action, and accountability. I hope you find this guided reclamation journal to be a supportive and transformational tool on your journey to achieve rest, your goals, your wildest dreams, and your life purpose. Enjoy the journey!

Please visit www.leidoswel.com to learn more and connect.

Open Letter to the Queen!

Welcome to Your Healing Journey, Sis!

This guided reclamation journal is a sacred companion to the book, *Navigating Rough S.E.A.S. — Soul Eroding Assimilation-Forcing Systems: A Playbook for Navigating Workplace Trauma and Reclaiming Power, Wellness, and Joy.*

The goal of this journal is to move from reading and feeling into the next level of doing and becoming. You are invited to reflect deeply, breathe intentionally, release what no longer serves you, and activate the fierce, phenomenal leader inside you.

As you move through each port of call, remember: healing is a process, not a race. It's a journey, not a destination. Take time to breathe and rest. Be intentional. Come back often.

Know that you are not alone. You are seen, heard, believed, supported, and celebrated. Sis, power, wellness, joy, and peace are around you and within you - embrace it!

Are you ready? Let's begin!

– Dr. T.

Table of Contents

"Your soul is your connection to your Creator and the most purest form of good. It must be protected and nourished at all times."

– Dr. T.

How To Use This Guided Reclamation Journal

Before we dive into this healing journey, let's get grounded. The images and symbols you will encounter throughout this journal, along with their meanings and purposes, are below.

Each chapter is divided into themes titled "Port of Calls." Similar to a cruise, these are stops intentionally created for your stretching, growth, and development.

Before any meaningful actions can be taken, we must first ground and locate ourselves. The Soul Compass sections were created for grounding reflections.

This symbol represents thinking and reflecting. These sections were created to allot additional space for reflecting on the topic at hand.

The Soul Assessment sections were created as an inventory tool to help you assess where you are currently in relation to where you would like to be in your leadership and life.

How To Use This Guided Reclamation Journal

The Deep Soul Diving sections are your invitation to go even deeper into your mind, body, and soul, and reflect on what is occurring beneath the surface.

Now that you have located, assessed, reflected, and dived deeper, the Reclaiming Her sections are an invitation for you to boldly embrace who you are and who you are striving to become.

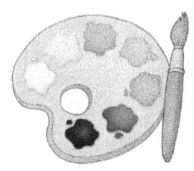

Art is a healing and positive coping strategy that calms the mind and engages the imagination. The Affirming Her Coloring Page sections were created with thoughtful images and affirmations.

The Debarkation sections mark the end of the "Port of Call." It offers an opportunity to highlight key takeaways, reflection summaries, and action steps before embarking on the next section or Port of Call.

How we speak to ourselves matters. What we believe about ourselves often determines our reality. The Sand Dollar Affirmation Bank is the place where you make deposits and withdrawals of positive and affirming words to remind yourself of who you are.

Anchoring Our Understanding

CLARIFYING TERMS

The words we use carry power — they shape how we see ourselves, how we see others, how we navigate systems, and how we reclaim what's been stolen, diminished, or silenced.

In this section, I offer terms not from a textbook — but from lived experience, cultural knowing, and a place of love and wellness. These are terms I invite you to sit with, challenge if needed, and navigate with a clear understanding.

The language in this guided reclamation journal is our compass for this journey. It's how we locate ourselves — and each other — as we navigate and heal from Rough S.E.A.S. — Soul Eroding Assimilation-Forcing Systems.

Anchoring Our Understanding

Soul

The soul is one of the deepest parts of our being. It's the place where our heart, mind, spirit, and body connect. The place where our mind, will, and emotions meet. The core of our humanity and being.

Eroding

Erosion is the slow and continuous degradation of a thing over time. In terms of humanity, the constant weathering or wearing down that slowly drains the energy and mindset essential for our thriving. If we are not diligent, we are often unaware of the weathering until it causes depletion.

Assimilation-forcing

Assimilation-forcing is being told (directly or indirectly) that you are not good enough as your whole authentic self. This results in being forced to hide, shrink, remove, or reject parts of your humanity, identity, culture, experiences, and values to be accepted or avoid negative consequences. Forced assimilation strips us of our freedom to choose.

Systems

Systems are a collection of policies, practices, and principles that work together to dictate how a particular thing operates and responds. Systems influence beliefs, behaviors, rewards, penalties, consequences, rights, and privileges. Systems ultimately impact the lives and outcomes of individuals, families, and communities. Systems are created, reinforced, and maintained by PEOPLE.

The Seven Waves of Rough S.E.A.S.™ Quiz

Throughout their careers, many Black women leaders encounter unique challenges in the workplace. Navigating Rough S.E.A.S. - Soul Eroding Assimilation-Forcing Systems is about identifying the impacts, overcoming and healing the effects of toxic workplace cultures, workplace abuse, and workplace trauma, and ultimately thriving.

There are seven phases or "waves" that Black women potentially experience as they are navigating workplace trauma and abuse. The Seven Waves of Rough S.E.A.S.™ is a model that highlights the phases of emotions employees navigate in the workplace. The model presents an impact continuum that encompasses both positive and negative experiences in the workplace.

The Seven Waves of Rough S.E.A.S. Quiz™ enables you to locate yourself by assessing which wave you are currently navigating. Once you identify your current wave, you are more likely to engage the resources and skills necessary to become unstuck physically, emotionally, and spiritually. It's essential to note that your waves may fluctuate over time, depending on your experiences with the organization, pivot plan, and your personal wellness strategies.

Armed with this knowledge and your copy of the Navigating Rough S.E.A.S. book and workbook, you can implement invaluable strategies and a plan of action for reclaiming your power, wellness, and joy through practical insights and actionable steps.

The Seven Waves of Rough S.E.A.S.™ Quiz

The link to the free quiz is provided below. Please note that this quiz is a component of a more comprehensive tool.

Link: https://www.leidoswel.com/7-waves-of-rough-seas

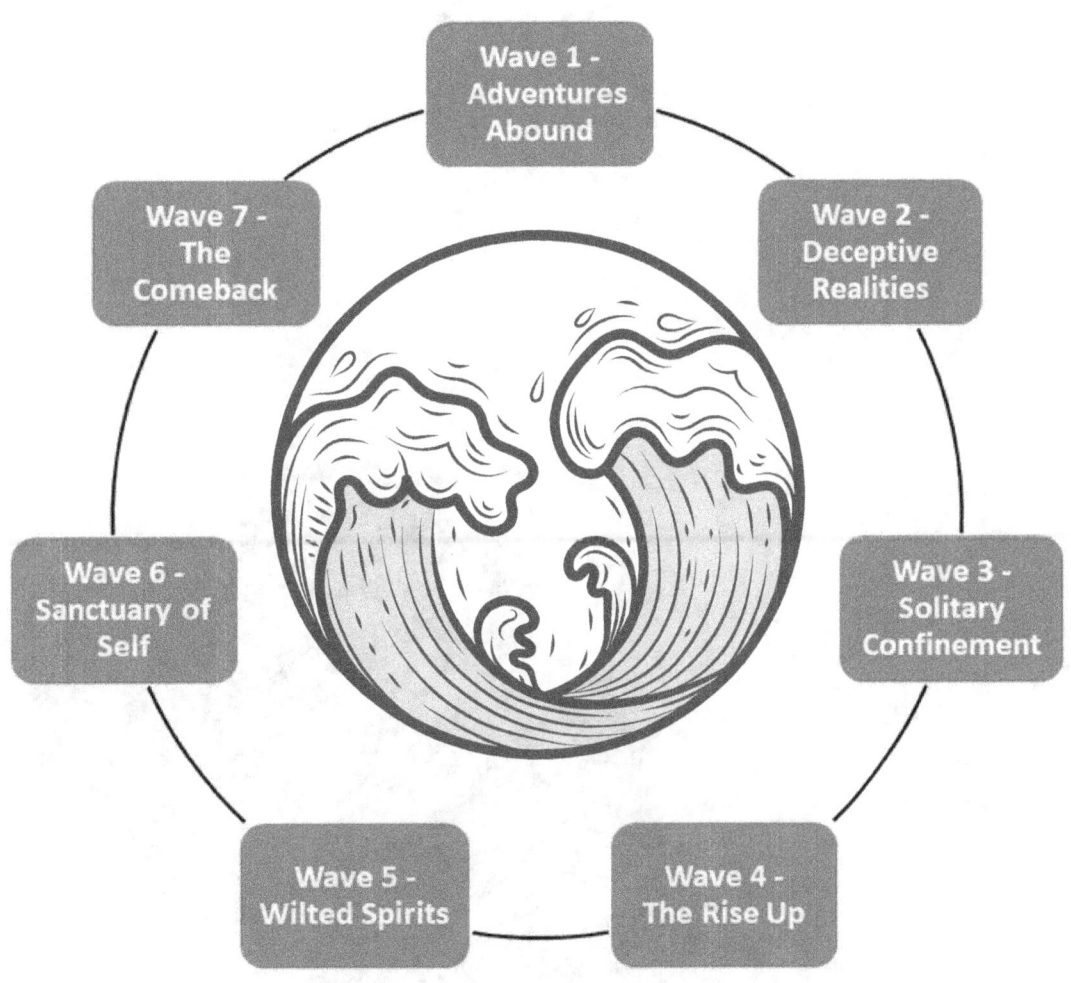

"Don't listen to those who say YOU CAN'T. Listen to the voice inside yourself that says, I CAN."

— Shirley Chisholm

Assessing The Condition of Your Soul

To Navigate Rough S.E.A.S., we must first assess and name what's been eroded — and what still remains.

Soul erosion occurs when systems or spaces ask us (explicitly or covertly) to abandon our authenticity, silence our truth, or contort ourselves to be accepted as the flavor of the day.

These experiences leave us disconnected from our bodies, our power, our wellness, and our joy. These experiences cause us to question our purpose and vision of who we are and what we were created to do in the world.

This section invites you to reflect gently and truthfully. It's not about reliving the pain — it's about honoring your truth so healing can occur.

SOUL COMPASS 1

Similar to the exercises in the book Navigating Rough S.E.A.S., the goal of the Soul Compass is to help you locate yourself and increase your self-awareness, so you can open your heart and mind to reflect courageously.

The times I feel most disconnected from my purpose and Creator.

A word that describes how my soul feels in this moment and why.

The beliefs, attitudes, and outlook that help me feel most connected.

Things I excel at when I feel aligned with my soul.

SOUL COMPASS REFLECTIONS

What thoughts and emotions came up for you as you were completing the Soul Compass activity? What surprised you? Did you notice any trends? Write your reflections below.

_____

_____

_____

_____

_____

_____

_____

_____

_____

_____

_____

_____

Removed - Remains - Recovered

The goal of this assessment is to self-audit. In the left column, list the things that have been removed, diminished, or taken in workplace settings. In the middle, list the parts of your being that have remained strong despite it all. On the right, list the things you desire to recover or rebuild.

What's Been Removed, Diminished, or Taken	What Still Remains Strong	What I Want To Recover or Rebuild

SOUL ASSESSMENT REFLECTIONS

What thoughts and emotions came up for you as you were completing the Soul Assessment activity? What surprised you? What actions will you take? Write your reflections below.

_____

_____

_____

_____

_____

_____

_____

_____

_____

_____

_____

DEEP SOUL DIVING 1

Choose one or more of these prompts to go deeper in your reflections. Write whatever comes up for you below.

• If my soul could speak without fear, what would it say about the systems I've survived.

• I am worthy of healing because…

• These parts of me are worthy of love, even if others rejected them…

_____

_____

_____

_____

_____

_____

_____

_____

_____

DEEP SOUL DIVING [CONT.]

_____

_____

_____

_____

_____

_____

_____

_____

_____

_____

_____

_____

_____

_____

_____

_____

RECLAIMING HER 1

Soul Re-Connection

A brief affirmation exercise to reconnect to your truth:

- Place your hand over your heart.

- Inhale slowly and exhale with a gentle sigh.

- Repeat silently or aloud: "I was created and chosen for a great purpose."

- Inhale slowly and exhale with a gentle sigh.

- Repeat silently or aloud: "I refuse to diminish myself or allow others to diminish me."

- Inhale slowly and exhale with a gentle sigh.

- Repeat silently or aloud: "I am enough, and I have enough resources around me to achieve my purpose in life."

- Listen — What does your soul want you to know today?

- Write it down.

RECLAIMING HER REFLECTIONS

What thoughts and emotions came up for you as you were engaging in the exercise? Write your reflections below.

_____

_____

_____

_____

_____

_____

_____

_____

_____

_____

_____

_____

SAND DOLLAR AFFIRMATION BANK 1

The affirmation bank is the place where you come to make deposits in yourself and make withdrawals to refill your well during challenging times. Consider the affirmations below as your starter account and add your own meaningful affirmation deposits.

Starter Account Affirmations

- My soul is not for sale. It is sacred and whole.
- I no longer trade my authenticity for approval.
- I will protect my soul from harmful internal and external forces.
- I will listen more intently to what my soul needs.

Your Affirmation Deposits

_____

_____

_____

_____

_____

_____

_____

AFFIRMING HER COLORING PAGE

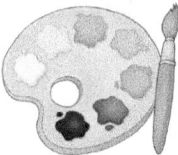

As you color this page, reflect on what grounds and replenishes you. What can you invite into your life today?

Even when I was made to feel invisible, my light remained.

Before moving on to the next port, ask yourself:

- What did I learn about myself?

- What emotions came up that I need to sit with or release?

- What do I want to carry forward from this port of call?

_____

_____

_____

_____

_____

_____

_____

_____

_____

_____

_____

"Some of your goals are buried so deep in fear it doesn't have access to what it needs to grow"
–Amanda Fludd

Who Are You At Your Core?

You are not their projection. You are your own reflection.

In soul-eroding systems, we are often made to feel that parts of our identity — our voice, expressions, hair, skin tone, style, name, cultural expressions — are wrong and must be muted to maintain "professionalism" or safety. We are led to believe that we must reshape who we were created to be to "climb the organizational ladder" and achieve success.

But true power begins with truthful identity.

This section helps you untangle the internalized messages you've received about who you had to be — and invites you to return to the woman you were created to be and become.

SOUL COMPASS 2

Similar to the book "Navigating Rough S.E.A.S.," the goal of the Soul Compass is to help you locate yourself and increase your self-awareness, so you can open your heart and mind to reflect courageously.

The first time I felt unseen, unsafe, or silenced in a professional space.

The parts of myself that I felt I had to hide to belong.

How have I been rewarded for shrinking — and what did it cost me?

What do I want to reclaim that I gave up?

SOUL COMPASS REFLECTIONS

What thoughts and emotions came up for you as you were completing the activity? What surprised you? What actions will you take? Write your reflections below.

_____

_____

_____

_____

_____

_____

_____

_____

_____

_____

_____

SOUL ASSESSMENT 2

Mirror, Mirror, Of My Soul

- Look in the mirror or close your eyes and envision your truest self — the version of you unimpacted by workplace assimilation, code-switching, or trauma.

- Now, use the space below to write a letter to her. Celebrate her. Commit to welcoming her back fully.

- Example Letter Starter Line:

    "Queen, I see you. Thank you for the support you have given me. I know I haven't always protected you well, but today I choose to honor your beauty, brilliance, perseverance, power, and truth by…"

_____

_____

_____

_____

_____

_____

_____

_____

SOUL ASSESSMENT REFLECTIONS

What thoughts and emotions came up for you as you were completing the Soul Assessment activity? How did it feel to reflect on this version of yourself? Write your reflections below.

_____

_____

_____

_____

_____

_____

_____

_____

_____

_____

_____

_____

DEEP SOUL DIVING 2

Choose one or more of these prompts to go deeper in your reflections. Write whatever comes up for you below.

- I have been taught to deny or suppress these parts of myself...

- When I show up fully as me, I feel...

- I want to always remember that I am...

_____

_____

_____

_____

_____

_____

_____

_____

_____

_____

DEEP SOUL DIVING [CONT.]

_____

_____

_____

_____

_____

_____

_____

_____

_____

_____

_____

_____

_____

_____

_____

_____

RECLAIMING HER 2

Identity Reclamation Bag

1. Find, draw, or imagine a purse or bag that represents you.

2. Place items, images, or memories inside that reflect your identity — photos, souvenirs/collectables, music, quotes, traditions, family photos, scents, fabrics, etc.

3. Each week, spend time with the box. Add to it. Reflect on how your truths and authentic self show up in your work and leadership.

4. Identify a reclamation statement and repeat it each time you visit your purse or bag. Example: "Today, I reclaim…"

RECLAIMING HER REFLECTIONS

What thoughts and emotions came up for you as you were completing the Reclaiming HER activity? What did you learn about yourself? What surprised you? Write your reflections below.

_____

_____

_____

_____

_____

_____

_____

_____

_____

_____

_____

_____

SAND DOLLAR AFFIRMATION BANK 2

The affirmation bank is the place where you come to make deposits in yourself and make withdrawals to refill your well during challenging times. Consider the affirmations below as your starter account and add your own meaningful affirmation deposits.

Starter Account Affirmations

- I'm not too much. I'm just enough for my calling.
- My purpose requires me to show up as my authentic self.
- I will no longer apologize for the power of my presence.
- There's someone who needs to see me walk in my power so they can embrace theirs.

Your Affirmation Deposits

_____

_____

_____

_____

_____

_____

_____

AFFIRMING HER COLORING PAGE

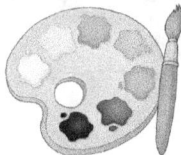

As you color this page, reflect on what grounds and replenishes you. What can you invite into your life today?

I'm no longer apologizing for the power of my presence.

Before moving on to the next port, ask yourself:

- What did I learn about myself?

- What emotions came up that I need to sit with or release?

- What do I want to carry forward from this port of call?

_____

_____

_____

_____

_____

_____

_____

_____

_____

_____

"What I will say is that what I've learned for myself is that I don't have to be anybody else and that myself is good enough; and that when I am being true to that self, then I can avail myself to extraordinary things. You have to allow for the impossible to be possible."
–Lupita Nyong'o

You Were Not Created To Blend In

Assimilation is not safety. It's slow self-erasure.

Many systems are designed to reward sameness and punish authenticity. For Black women leaders, assimilation can feel like the price of access. But every time we silence our truth, overperform to prove our worth, or strip away our cultural expressions to 'fit in,' we make a withdrawal from our soul.

In this section, we'll confront the systems that taught us to conform — and begin reclaiming the power of our unapologetic presence.

SOUL COMPASS 3

Similar to the book "Navigating Rough S.E.A.S.," the goal of the Soul Compass is to help you locate yourself and increase your self-awareness, so you can open your heart and mind to reflect courageously.

The spoken or unspoken workplace rules that have forced me to assimilate.

How does the assimilated version of myself experience the workplace?

What am I modeling for others, both inside and outside of my workplace?

What would it feel like to belong without betraying myself?

SOUL COMPASS REFLECTIONS

What thoughts and emotions came up for you as you were completing the Soul Compass activity? What surprised you? How are you being impacted? Write your reflections below.

_____

_____

_____

_____

_____

_____

_____

_____

_____

_____

_____

_____

SOUL ASSESSMENT 3

Disrupting Negative Narratives

- On the following page, draw three concentric circles labeled:

  "Me" → "My Workplace Culture" → "The System"

- In each circle, write or draw:

  ○ **Me:** Ways you've adjusted your voice, dress, tone, values

  ○ **Workplace Culture:** Common behaviors, language, or expectations (e.g., "keep it light," "be a team player," "don't make it racial," "don't be angry," "we're like family")

  ○ **The System:** Cultural or societal messages about race, gender, power, and success in the workplace (e.g., "you should have all the answers," "don't mess things up for the next Black person," "hustle until you die," "be humble")

- Now:

  ○ Draw a **square** around the systemic messages that have influenced your workplace.

  ○ Draw an **asterisk** next to the workplace messages that have shaped you.

  ○ Draw a **line through** the messages or behaviors you are letting go of.

SOUL ASSESSMENT REFLECTIONS

What thoughts and emotions came up for you as you were completing the activity? What surprised you? What actions will you take? Write your reflections below.

_____

_____

_____

_____

_____

_____

_____

_____

_____

_____

_____

_____

DEEP SOUL DIVING 3

Choose one or more of these prompts to go deeper in your reflections. Write whatever comes up for you below.

- I must unlearn these oppressive narratives...

- I believe I am, and I am becoming...

- I will hold myself accountable to my authenticity because...

_____

_____

_____

_____

_____

_____

_____

_____

_____

DEEP SOUL DIVING [CONT.]

_____

_____

_____

_____

_____

_____

_____

_____

_____

_____

_____

_____

_____

_____

_____

RECLAIMING HER 3

Powerful Reprogramming

Loading...

Oftentimes, our brains run negative narratives on autopilot. Here are a few short, powerful scripts you can say (or remind yourself of) the next time you feel pressured to shrink, overcompensate, code-switch, or assimilate.

Examples:

• "I'd like to offer a different perspective that reflects my experiences."

• "I need a moment to process this in a way that honors my values."

• "I'm here to participate as my full self."

Write your own below. Then practice saying them in the mirror.

_____

_____

_____

_____

_____

RECLAIMING HER REFLECTIONS

What thoughts and emotions came up for you as you were completing the activity? What did you learn about yourself? What actions will you take? Write your reflections below.

_____

_____

_____

_____

_____

_____

_____

_____

_____

_____

_____

_____

SAND DOLLAR AFFIRMATION BANK 3

The affirmation bank is the place where you come to make deposits in yourself and make withdrawals to refill your well during challenging times. Consider the affirmations below as your starter account and add your own meaningful affirmation deposits.

Starter Account Affirmations

- I don't owe assimilation to anyone.
- I am not too loud, too Black, too bold — I am just right.
- I will no longer allow my passion and care to be weaponized against me.
- My anger does not mean I am unhinged.

Your Affirmation Deposits

_____

_____

_____

_____

_____

_____

_____

AFFIRMING HER COLORING PAGE

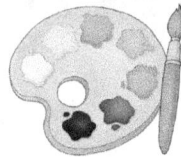

As you color this page, reflect on what grounds and replenishes you. What can you invite into your life today?

I'm unlearning the rules that were never mine to carry.

Before moving on to the next port, ask yourself:

- What did I learn about myself?

- What do I need to unlearn?

- What do I want to carry forward from this port of call?

_____

_____

_____

_____

_____

_____

_____

_____

_____

_____

_____

"It's time for you to move, realizing that the thing you are seeking is also seeking you."
– Iyanla Vanzant

Back and Better Than Before!

You are not returning to who you used to be. You are soaring into who you were created to become.

Reclaiming your soul doesn't mean going back to the version of you that existed before the harm. It means rising into a new, evolved, whole version of yourself — one who leads with clarity, joy, power, and unapologetic truth.

This section is a sacred homecoming. A remembering. A return to joy and power that has always been your birthright.

SOUL COMPASS 4

Similar to the book "Navigating Rough S.E.A.S.," the goal of the Soul Compass is to help you locate yourself and increase your self-awareness, so you can open your heart and mind to reflect courageously.

The new truths I'm living in, now that I've named the harm and chosen myself.

The parts of myself I am determined to reclaim throughout my journey.

What does liberation feel like in my mind? In my body? In my soul?

How will I protect the things I've reclaimed or built?

SOUL COMPASS REFLECTIONS

What thoughts and emotions came up for you as you were completing the Soul Compass activity? What surprised you? What actions will you take? Write your reflections below.

_____

_____

_____

_____

_____

_____

_____

_____

_____

_____

_____

_____

SOUL ASSESSMENT 4

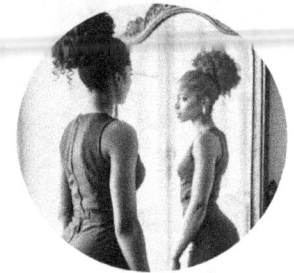

The Joy Honeycomb

Use the honeycomb below to add words, symbols, or images that reflect what joy means to you and your life:

- Moments when you felt most alive
- People, spaces, things, or practices that restore you
- Dreams that still ignite your spirit and make your heart smile
- Future visions of joy in your leadership and life

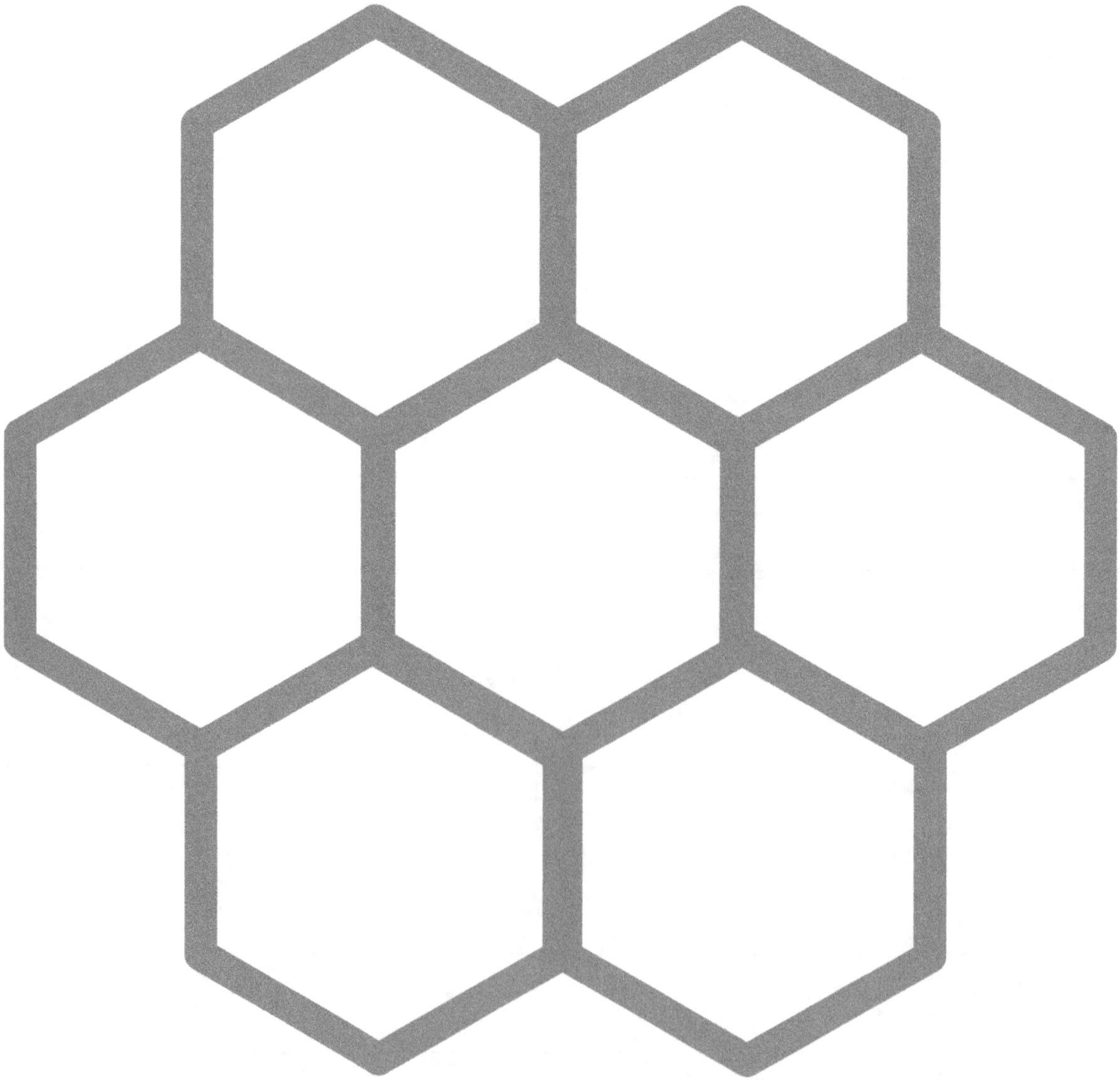

SOUL ASSESSMENT REFLECTIONS

What thoughts and emotions came up for you as you were completing the activity? What surprised you? What's making your heart smile in this moment? Write your reflections below.

_____

_____

_____

_____

_____

_____

_____

_____

_____

_____

_____

_____

_____

DEEP SOUL DIVING 4

Choose one or more of these prompts to go deeper in your reflections. Write whatever comes up for you below.

• This is what joy looks like when I'm no longer surviving...

• I choose to lead with love because...

• I feel powerful when...

_____

_____

_____

_____

_____

_____

_____

_____

_____

DEEP SOUL DIVING [CONT.]

Create a Joy Routine

Design a daily or weekly ritual that centers your joy. Here are some examples. Write yours below.

• Light a candle and play your favorite song.

• Speak five affirmations aloud.

• Move your body in gratitude.

• Journal one joy moment from the day.

• Sip your favorite tea while painting or coloring.

_____

_____

_____

_____

_____

RECLAIMING HER REFLECTIONS

What thoughts and emotions came up for you as you were completing the activity? What did you learn about yourself? What brings you the most joy? Write your reflections below.

_____

_____

_____

_____

_____

_____

_____

_____

_____

_____

_____

_____

SAND DOLLAR AFFIRMATION BANK 4

The affirmation bank is the place where you come to make deposits in yourself and make withdrawals to refill your well during challenging times. Consider the affirmations below as your starter account and add your own meaningful affirmation deposits.

Starter Account Affirmations

- I am joy.
- There is no part of me that must be left behind to soar.
- I can choose to change my mind and make new decisions today.
- I can and will choose ME.

Your Affirmation Deposits

_____

_____

_____

_____

_____

_____

AFFIRMING HER COLORING PAGE

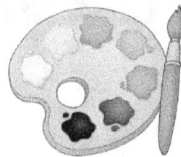

As you color this page, reflect on what grounds and replenishes you. What can you invite into your life today?

My joy is resistance, resilience, and rebirth.

Before moving on to the next port, ask yourself:

- What does it mean to live in my reclaimed joy?

- What emotions came up that I need to sit with or release?

- What do I want to carry forward from this port of call?

_____

_____

_____

_____

_____

_____

_____

_____

_____

_____

"The most common way people give up their power is by thinking they don't have any."
–Alice Walker

Stand In Your Power, Unapologetically

Power is not what they give you — it's what you reclaim each time you lead from your truth.

Reclaiming power doesn't mean replicating oppressive systems. It means showing up rooted in your values, voice, and vision — with boundaries, clarity, and joy. Power lives within you; you just have to embrace it and use it.

This section is about owning your story, embodying your power, and declaring: "I am the captain of my success!"

SOUL COMPASS 5

Similar to the book "Navigating Rough S.E.A.S.," the goal of the Soul Compass is to help you locate yourself and increase your self-awareness, so you can open your heart and mind to reflect courageously.

How do I define my power beyond my title, role, perks, salary, and organization?	Places and spaces in my life and leadership where I have felt the most powerful.

How I want others to experience my leadership power.	The values that I will anchor my leadership in moving forward.

SOUL COMPASS REFLECTIONS

What thoughts and emotions came up for you as you were completing the Soul Compass activity? What surprised you? How are you using your power? Write your reflections below.

_____

_____

_____

_____

_____

_____

_____

_____

_____

_____

_____

_____

SOUL ASSESSMENT 5

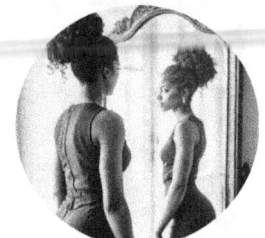

My Leadership Legacy

Use the image below to outline your leadership legacy. Include images, words, colors, and symbols that inspire you to lead boldly as you embrace your power, wellness, joy, and purpose.

- **Foundation:** Core values that ground your leadership
- **Middle:** Lived experiences and wisdom that inform your voice
- **Top:** Your leadership vision, legacy, and impact

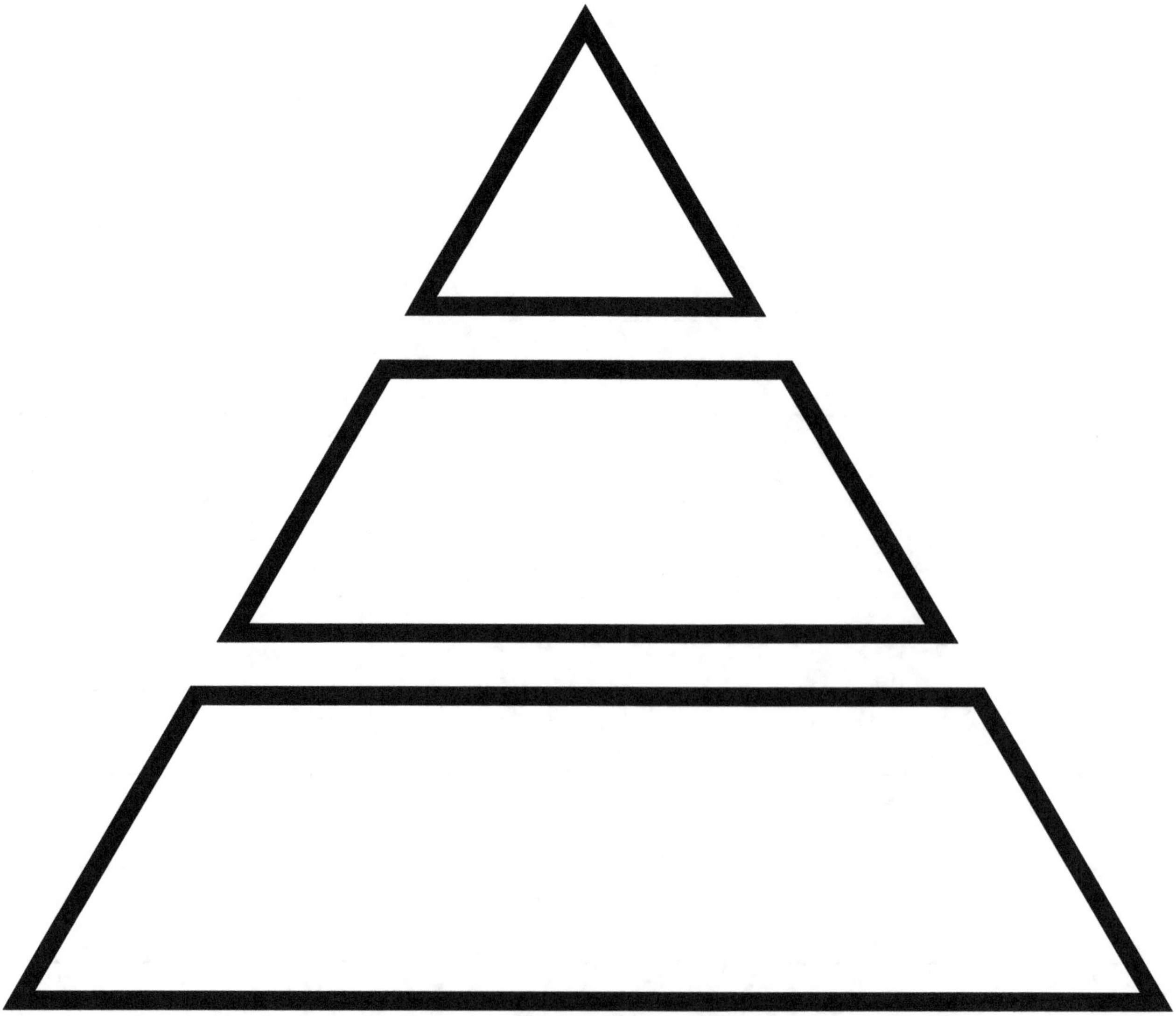

SOUL ASSESSMENT REFLECTIONS

What thoughts and emotions came up for you as you were completing the activity? What surprised you? What is your leadership legacy? Write your reflections below.

_____

_____

_____

_____

_____

_____

_____

_____

_____

_____

_____

_____

_____

DEEP SOUL DIVING 5

Choose one or more of these prompts to go deeper in your reflections. Write whatever comes up for you below.

• Power feels like this in my body...

• I will use my leadership power to (or for)...

• I continue to show up as my whole, powerful self by...

_____

_____

_____

_____

_____

_____

_____

_____

_____

DEEP SOUL DIVING [CONT.]

_____

_____

_____

_____

_____

_____

_____

_____

_____

_____

_____

_____

_____

_____

RECLAIMING HER 5

Leadership Power Agreement

Develop a leadership power agreement between you and your higher self. Include the following items and add others as you see fit.

- Your personal leadership power mission statement

- Core leadership values

- Boundaries you will uphold

- Your power, wellness, and joy-centered leadership vision

- Signature + optional witness (coach, sister-friend, or trusted peer)

_____

_____

_____

_____

RECLAIMING HER 5
Leadership Power Agreement

_____

_____

_____

_____

_____

_____

_____

_____

_____

_____

_____

_____

_____

_____

_____

_____

_____

_____

_____

_____

_____

Signed In Power & Liberation: _____ Date: _____

Accountability Partner: _____ Date: _____

RECLAIMING HER REFLECTIONS

What thoughts and emotions came up for you as you were completing the activity? What did you learn about yourself? What surprised you? Write your reflections below.

_____

_____

_____

_____

_____

_____

_____

_____

_____

_____

_____

_____

SAND DOLLAR AFFIRMATION BANK 5

The affirmation bank is the place where you come to make deposits in yourself and make withdrawals to refill your well during challenging times. Consider the affirmations below as your starter account and add your own meaningful affirmation deposits.

Starter Account Affirmations

- I am a leader rooted in truth, not performance.
- I don't shrink to lead — I rise and shine vibrantly.
- I am powerful beyond my wildest dreams and imagination.
- I will not allow the power I possess to be in vain or underutilized.

Your Affirmation Deposits

_____

_____

_____

_____

_____

_____

AFFIRMING HER COLORING PAGE

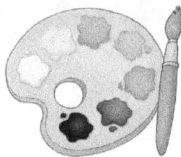

As you color this page, reflect on what grounds and replenishes you. What can you invite into your life today?

![Coloring page illustration of a woman sitting on the edge of a bed with her hands pressed together in prayer]

My leadership honors my ancestors, my values, and my vision.

Before moving on to the next port, ask yourself:

- What did I learn about myself?

- How will I honor my power every single day?

- What do I want to carry forward from this port of call?

_____

_____

_____

_____

_____

_____

_____

_____

_____

_____

"You don't always have to be doing something. Doing nothing is doing something, too. Prioritize your wellness by choice, or it will make you prioritize it by force."

– Dr. T.

The Power of Wellness

I belong. I don't have to burn out to prove I belong. I am worthy of rest, healing, wellness, joy, and ease.

Systems of assimilation and overperformance have taught us to neglect our bodies, deny our needs, and call burnout success. But true leadership begins with holistic wellness.

Reclaiming your wellness means giving yourself permission to care for your mind, body, and spirit without guilt. It means refilling your well before pouring into others.

Wellness is your right. Not because you've done enough, but because you are enough.

SOUL COMPASS 6

Similar to the book "Navigating Rough S.E.A.S.," the goal of the Soul Compass is to help you locate yourself and increase your self-awareness, so you can open your heart and mind to reflect courageously.

The messages I have internalized about rest, self-care, or asking for help.

How does stress show up in my body — and how do I respond?

Wellness practices that nourish me and align with my authentic self.

How do I show up when I am highly well in my mind, body, soul, and spirit?

SOUL COMPASS REFLECTIONS

What thoughts and emotions came up for you as you were completing the activity? How does wellness show up in your life and leadership? Write your reflections below.

_____

_____

_____

_____

_____

_____

_____

_____

_____

_____

_____

_____

Wellness Check-In

Use the chart below to assess your current state of wellness across key dimensions. Be honest — this is not about judgment, but awareness.

Area	Current Feeling	Desired Feeling	One Action I Can Take To Achieve or Maintain My Desired Feeling
Mental Wellness			
Emotional Balance			
Social Connection			
Physical Wellness			
Spiritual Connection			
Financial Wellness			

SOUL ASSESSMENT REFLECTIONS

What thoughts and emotions came up for you as you were completing the activity? What's one action step from your list that you will take this week? Write your reflections below.

_____

_____

_____

_____

_____

_____

_____

_____

_____

_____

_____

_____

DEEP SOUL DIVING 6

Choose one or more of these prompts to go deeper in your reflections. Write whatever comes up for you below.

• Wellness feels like this in my body...

• I am most at peace when...

• These are the ways I will honor my body and boundaries...

• I am learning to trust my body's signals because...

_____

_____

_____

_____

_____

_____

_____

_____

_____

DEEP SOUL DIVING [CONT.]

_____

_____

_____

_____

_____

_____

_____

_____

_____

_____

_____

_____

_____

_____

_____

RECLAIMING HER 6

Weekly Wellness Practice

Create a wellness practice that reconnects you to your breath, body, soul, and boundaries. Examples may include the following. You can use the spaces below to add your own practices.

• Morning stillness before emails

• 10-minute evening stretch with affirmations

• Drinking water throughout the day

• Taking time to eat breakfast and lunch away from your work

• Saying "No" and not explaining why

• Lighting a candle for yourself at the end of the week and reflecting on your successes, wins, and gratitudes

_____

_____

_____

_____

RECLAIMING HER REFLECTIONS

What thoughts and emotions came up for you as you were completing the activity? What wellness practices will you focus on and prioritize this week? Write your reflections below.

_____

_____

_____

_____

_____

_____

_____

_____

_____

_____

_____

_____

_____

SAND DOLLAR AFFIRMATION BANK 6

The affirmation bank is the place where you come to make deposits in yourself and make withdrawals to refill your well during challenging times. Consider the affirmations below as your starter account and add your own meaningful affirmation deposits.

Starter Account Affirmations

- My body is not a battleground — it is a sanctuary.
- Wellness is my self-fullness — it's how I show up replenished and whole.
- I honor my healing as a daily act of power.
- I will listen to my body and will not override its signals.

Your Affirmation Deposits

_____

_____

_____

_____

_____

_____

_____

AFFIRMING HER COLORING PAGE

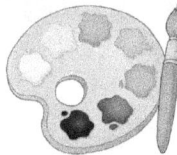

As you color this page, reflect on what grounds and replenishes you. What can you invite into your life today?

I am not a machine. I am a living, breathing soul deserving of rest.

Before moving on to the next port, ask yourself:

- What do I need more of in my wellness journey?

- What boundaries will I set or reinforce to protect my wellness?

- What do I want to carry forward from this port of call?

_____

_____

_____

_____

_____

_____

_____

_____

_____

_____

_____

"Radical joy isn't just a pursuit; it's an act of defiance. A reclamation of our right to thrive in the face of systems that seek to diminish us."

— Malebo Sephodi

This Joy That I Have, The World Can't Take It Away!

Joy is not a luxury. Joy is liberation.

In systems that thrive on burnout, trauma, and urgency, our joy is often dismissed, suppressed, or forgotten. But joy is our sacred inheritance.

This section invites you to reclaim joy not just as a moment, but as a mindset, a movement, and as medicine.

You are worthy of joy now. Not when you've earned it. Not when everything is perfect.

NOW!

SOUL COMPASS 7

Similar to the book "Navigating Rough S.E.A.S.," the goal of the Soul Compass is to help you locate yourself and increase your self-awareness, so you can open your heart and mind to reflect courageously.

The people, places, and things that bring me joy.

Beliefs I have internalized about joy. Which are harmful? Which are helpful?

The last time I felt pure, unfiltered joy, what was occurring?

What would it look, sound, and feel like to prioritize joy in my leadership?

SOUL COMPASS REFLECTIONS

What thoughts and emotions came up for you as you were completing the activity? What surprised you? How do you ignite joy in your life? Write your reflections below.

_____

_____

_____

_____

_____

_____

_____

_____

_____

_____

_____

_____

Use the chart below to reflect on what brings you joy in different areas of your life. This will help you reconnect with your whole self.

Area	What Brings Me Joy
Body & Movement	
Mind & Creativity	
Relationships	
Spiritually	
Purpose	
Work/Career	

SOUL ASSESSMENT REFLECTIONS

What thoughts and emotions came up for you as you were completing the activity? What surprised you? What area are you most joyful in? Write your reflections below.

_____

_____

_____

_____

_____

_____

_____

_____

_____

_____

_____

_____

_____

DEEP SOUL DIVING 7

Choose one or more of these prompts to go deeper in your reflections. Write whatever comes up for you below.

- The meaning of joy in my life…

- When I feel my joy is running low, I can do this…

- I deserve joy because…

_____

_____

_____

_____

_____

_____

_____

_____

_____

DEEP SOUL DIVING [CONT.]

_____

_____

_____

_____

_____

_____

_____

_____

_____

_____

_____

_____

_____

_____

_____

_____

_____

RECLAIMING HER 7

Creating A Joy Jar

- Use slips of colorful paper or sticky notes

- Each day, or at least once a week, briefly write about one joyful
    - moment,
    - compliment,
    - win, or
    - smile-worthy occasion or reflection

- Pull from the jar on tough days to remind yourself: joy is always present — even during the storms.

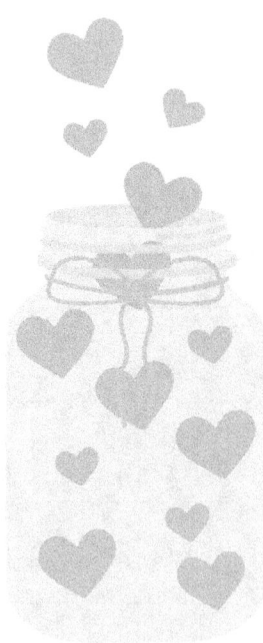

RECLAIMING HER REFLECTIONS

What thoughts and emotions came up for you as you were thinking about your joy jar? When will you begin designing and implementing your joy jar? Write your reflections below.

_____

_____

_____

_____

_____

_____

_____

_____

_____

_____

_____

_____

SAND DOLLAR AFFIRMATION BANK 7

The affirmation bank is the place where you come to make deposits in yourself and make withdrawals to refill your well during challenging times. Consider the affirmations below as your starter account and add your own meaningful affirmation deposits.

Starter Account Affirmations

- I give myself full permission to experience joy without guilt.
- My joy is my divine right.
- My joy is worth fighting for.
- Joy is how I heal my mind, body, and soul.

Your Affirmation Deposits

_____

_____

_____

_____

_____

_____

AFFIRMING HER COLORING PAGE

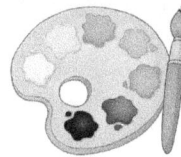

As you color this page, reflect on what grounds and replenishes you. What can you invite into your life today?

I don't have to earn joy. I just have to receive it.

Before moving on to the next port, ask yourself:

- What did I learn about myself?

- What will I do to protect my joy going forward?

- What do I want to carry forward from this port of call?

_____

_____

_____

_____

_____

_____

_____

_____

_____

_____

_____

"For me, becoming isn't about arriving somewhere or achieving a certain aim. I see it instead as forward motion, a means of evolving, a way to reach continuously toward a better self. The journey doesn't end."
– Michelle Obama

Lead Fiercely

You are not here to fit into broken leadership models. You are here to build new ones, rooted in justice, joy, love, and truth.

Too often, leadership is defined by titles, proximity to power, and a willingness to out and over perform. But reclaimed leadership starts within — grounded in balance, boundaries, integrity, identity, love, and embodied values.

This section invites you to redefine leadership on your own terms. Not who they said you had to be, but who you are when you boldly lead fully in your skin, with courage, compassion, love, and clarity.

This section is about owning your story, embodying your leadership, and declaring: "I will lead in my skin. And I will win."

SOUL COMPASS 8

Similar to the book "Navigating Rough S.E.A.S.," the goal of the Soul Compass is to help you locate yourself and increase your self-awareness, so you can open your heart and mind to reflect courageously.

Beliefs I have internalized about what it means to be a good leader.

What are my leadership values? What do I stand for and stand on?

Leadership qualities I naturally embody and take pride in.

Times when I feel most effective or authentic as a leader.

SOUL COMPASS REFLECTIONS

What thoughts and emotions came up for you as you were completing the activity? What surprised you? How can you improve? Write your reflections below.

_____

_____

_____

_____

_____

_____

_____

_____

_____

_____

_____

_____

SOUL ASSESSMENT 8

The True Leader Within Me

Use the chart below to reflect on assimilation-forcing leadership expectations and the intersections between your leadership values. This will help you reconnect with your authentic self and leadership.

I've been told to lead like this...	But I want to lead like this...

SOUL ASSESSMENT REFLECTIONS

What thoughts and emotions came up for you as you were completing the activity? What surprised you about your values? What must you unlearn? Write your reflections below.

_____

_____

_____

_____

_____

_____

_____

_____

_____

_____

_____

DEEP SOUL DIVING 8

Choose one or more of these prompts to go deeper in your reflections. Write whatever comes up for you below.

- When I lead in alignment with my truth, I feel...

- How I want my leadership to be felt and experienced by others...

- The impact I want my leadership to make in this world......

_____

_____

_____

_____

_____

_____

_____

_____

_____

_____

DEEP SOUL DIVING [CONT.]

_____

_____

_____

_____

_____

_____

_____

_____

_____

_____

_____

_____

_____

_____

RECLAIMING HER 8
My Liberated Leadership Manifesto

- Using the following page, write your Liberated Leadership Manifesto — a bold declaration of how you choose to lead.

- It should reflect your purpose, your values, your voice, and your vision.

- It should include your plan for honoring and protecting your power, wellness, joy, rest, and peace.

- Use these sentence starters if you need ideas:

    ○ I lead from a place of…

    ○ I reject leadership ideals that require me to…

    ○ The people I lead can expect…

    ○ I am not here to prove — I am here to…

RECLAIMING HER 8

My Liberated Leadership Manifesto

_____
_____
_____
_____
_____
_____
_____
_____
_____
_____
_____
_____
_____
_____
_____
_____
_____
_____
_____
_____
_____

Signed In Power & Liberation: _____   Date: _____

RECLAIMING HER REFLECTIONS

What thoughts and emotions came up for you as you were completing the activity? How will you hold yourself accountable? Write your reflections below.

_____

_____

_____

_____

_____

_____

_____

_____

_____

_____

_____

_____

_____

SAND DOLLAR AFFIRMATION BANK 8

The affirmation bank is the place where you come to make deposits in yourself and make withdrawals to refill your well during challenging times. Consider the affirmations below as your starter account and add your own meaningful affirmation deposits.

Starter Account Affirmations

- My leadership doesn't have to look like theirs to be powerful.
- I lead in my skin — with courage, boundaries, and joy.
- I do not perform. I embody healthy leadership.
- I create transformative ripple effects in every room I enter.

Your Affirmation Deposits

_____

_____

_____

_____

_____

_____

_____

AFFIRMING HER COLORING PAGE

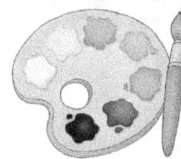

As you color this page, reflect on what grounds and replenishes you. What can you invite into your life today?

I lead with integrity and joy every day.

Before moving on to the next port, ask yourself:

- What did I learn about myself?

- What new leadership story am I writing for myself?

- What do I want to carry forward from this port of call?

- What is one powerful, liberating way I will lead this week?

_____

_____

_____

_____

_____

_____

_____

_____

_____

_____

"If you are always trying to be normal, you will never know how amazing you can be."

– Maya Angelou

Let's Go, Sis!

You did it! You completed the journal!

This guided reclamation journal is just the beginning. The healing, power, wellness, joy, and peace you've reclaimed here will continue to grow as you nurture yourself and build communities that uplift your truth. Take a moment to celebrate that! These are sacred gifts you can carry into every space you occupy.

You are powerful. You are worthy. You are enough. Your liberation and evolution journey continues — through your leadership, your community, and your radiant presence.

Remember to return this journal whenever you need grounding, guidance, or a reminder of the fierce leader you are becoming. Keep speaking, healing, loving, and leading in your skin — because the world needs your light.

Thank you for allowing yourself to be seen, heard, celebrated, and healed. Thank you for taking the time to prioritize YOU! I am honored to be on this path with you!

Keep soaring, Sis!

With Great Love & Gratitude,

– Dr. T.

About Dr. Tonicia Freeman-Foster

Dr. Tonicia Freeman-Foster, also known as Dr. T. or Dr. TF^2 is the best-selling author of Navigating Rough S.E.A.S. — Soul Eroding Assimilation-Forcing Systems: A Playbook for Navigating Workplace Trauma and Reclaiming Power, Wellness, and Joy. She serves as the Co-Founder and CEO of LEIDOSWEL —a firm specializing in leadership development coaching and consulting for mid- to executive-level leaders and entrepreneurs nationwide.

With over 20 years of leadership experience, Dr. T. believes that leadership is a muscle that requires continuous exercise and lifelong learning. She has a healthy obsession with all things leadership, including a Master's and Doctorate degree in leadership concentrations. She is passionate about curating spaces and communities for leaders, especially for Black women leaders, to thrive authentically.

Dr. T. takes pride in working with leaders nationally and helping them achieve their full potential. As a reclamation coach, Dr. T. helps leaders who are struggling with negative self-talk, confidence challenges, and fear, so they can achieve their goals and confidently lead their teams to wild success. As a consultant, she supports organizations in cultivating cultures where staff, clients, patients, and communities are engaged and thrive equitably.

Please visit www.leidoswel.com to learn more and connect.

LET'S WORK TOGETHER!

- Do you feel stuck in your leadership as a result of fear, Imposter Syndrome, negative self-talk, low confidence, past workplace trauma, or a lack of new skills?

- Can you imagine how powerful your leadership could be if you could just unleash it fully?

Imagine what work could look and feel like if you had your own personal coach to see you, listen to you, challenge you, cheer you on, support you with effective leadership tools, and help you soar in your role and beyond. Well, the wait is over!

Lead In Your Skin & Win is a coaching experience that supports leaders in becoming UNstuck so they can navigate challenges, achieve their goals, and lead their teams to wild success!

Sunkissed Sunflower Queens is a leadership development community created to support the unique needs of mid- to executive-level Black women leaders and entrepreneurs. It is a healing community where Black women leaders and entrepreneurs are seen, heard, celebrated, and supported authentically with the tools necessary to thrive.

For more information about these experiences and to schedule your free consultation, please visit: www.leidoswel.com

LET'S CONNECT!

Join Our Newsletter Community

www.leidoswel.com

Podcast: Reclaiming HER Leadership

Apple Podcast, iHeart, Spotify

LinkedIn

www.linkedin.com/in/toniciaff

YouTube

www.youtube.com/@dr.toniciafreeman-foster7600

Instagram

www.instagram.com/leidoswel

Email

info@leidoswel.com